CW01084727

CONTENTS

WELCOME!

This book is a short introduction to the basics of our Christian faith. We hope that by reading it you will learn new things, understand things that had confused you before, and be reminded of things you'd forgotten. But while learning and understanding are important, this book is also about living and doing and, perhaps most vitally, relating — relating to the God of love who is at the centre of everything that is written in the pages that follow.

So, although this book contains some stories, some references to movies and celebrities, and some great graphics, we hope that you will not read it like a glossy, gossipy magazine — a fun treat but with no lasting benefits. And, although there are some facts, some technical terms and some reasoning, we hope you will not read this book like an academic textbook — filling your head with knowledge for an exam on Friday but forgotten by Monday. Instead, because this book is about the Christian faith – an exciting, life-giving, world-changing, destiny-determining relationship with the living God – we hope that it will challenge you to live your whole life a little differently and, especially, to enjoy your relationship with God to the maximum.

'I HAVE COME THAT THEY MAY HAVE LIFE, AND HAVE IT TO THE FULL.' JOHN 10:10

READ ON
ROMANS 12:1–2

While some of us are converts to Christianity, many of us have grown up in the Church as part of a Christian family. Some of our earliest memories are of singing *If I were a fuzzy-wuzzy bear* and of watching puppet shows about Jesus feeding the 5,000, or Jonah being swallowed then coughed-up by a great fish. So it's reasonable to ask, 'If we've been Christians for a while, if we are old hands at church-going and well schooled in Bible stories, then why do we need to bother with the basics?'

Well, for a start, church is not the only (or even the biggest) influence on our lives. Most of us live in towns and cities that we share with people from many different parts of the world. Among our friends and neighbours we will find many different views of what life is all about. On our high streets and in our high schools there are many different and competing moralities (Is it right to kill animals for food or for scientific experimentation or should they be treated as persons with their own rights?), many different and competing beliefs (Will I be reincarnated when I die or will I cease to exist?) and many different understandings of the nature of the world (Was it formed by physical processes alone or was a divine creator involved?). Moving from actual reality to virtual reality, the range of opinions and influences expands even further – everyone is allowed to have their say and anyone is able to listen. Our faith is inevitably coloured by this weird and wonderful culture we live in. So, we need to take time and make a conscious effort to learn to think and to act like Christians, to enjoy our relationship with God and enjoy the abundant, exciting and challenging life that He wants us to live.

Some people (occasionally and unkindly called geeks, nerds or anoraks) have the knack of combining encyclopaedic knowledge of something – football, for example – with a total lack of ability to actually do it. These are the people who could tell you who scored every goal in   >>

an exciting, life-giving, world-changing, destiny-determining relationship with the living God

translate their learning about
God into living for God

every match of the 1986 FA Cup third round, but would take a divot the size of a small island out of the pitch and end up lying on their backs with their feet in the air, if they actually tried to kick a ball. Similarly, throughout history (and possibly in our churches today), there have been Christians who knew everything there was to know about theology, doctrine and the Bible, and yet lived lives that were dry, unattractive and sometimes downright evil. Unsurprisingly, these people failed to please either God or their peers.

The Christian faith isn't about intellectual brilliance or memorisation of key doctrines any more than football is about statistics and history. What pleases God, impacts society and draws outsiders to Christ, is the way Christians live. Being able to translate their learning about God into living for God has enabled Christians throughout history to live flourishing, beautiful lives and, when necessary, to die brave deaths. With that in mind, the ten chapters of this book aim to offer you teaching combined with practical ideas for action – the learning and the living are woven together.

Each of the first six chapters begins with learning – focusing on the things that the Bible and Christian doctrine teach us about God, His acts and His plans and purposes – but finishes by looking at the impact that knowledge should have on our day-to-day lives.

The final four sessions begin with the way life can be lived according to God's plan and in His power – but conclude with a short thought on what the lifestyle we are called to teaches us about God.

But that's just the way the book's written. Far more important is the way the book's read – by you! To make the most of this book it should be read carefully, prayerfully and actively. When you come across something that interests you or challenges you, take some time to read the suggested Bible passages, to pray about what you've read and, most important of all, to consider how your lifestyle (your way of thinking, acting and relating) should change as a result.

A PASSIONATE DESIRE

Those of us who have been involved in the production of this book have a passionate desire that you might be helped to know God more truly, invited to experience His love more deeply and strengthened to live for Him more vibrantly. No one has ever expressed this desire more passionately or more eloquently than the apostle Paul, so we will close this welcoming chapter with the words of his prayer for the Ephesians; this is also our prayer.

For this reason I kneel before the Father, from whom his whole family in heaven and on earth derives its name. I pray that out of his glorious riches he may strengthen you with power through his Spirit in your inner being, so that Christ may dwell in your hearts through faith. And I pray that you, being rooted and established in love, may have power, together with all the saints, to grasp how wide and long and high and deep is the love of Christ, and to know this love that surpasses knowledge – that you may be filled to the measure of all the fulness of God.

Now to him who is able to do immeasurably more than all we ask or imagine, according to his power that is at work within us, to him be glory in the church and in Christ Jesus throughout all generations, for ever and ever! Amen. (Eph. 3:14–21)

ONE :GOD

ALMOST EVERYONE
BELIEVES IN SOME
KIND OF GOD.
THE QUESTION IS:

HOW CAN WE KNOW WHA
GOD IS
REALLY
LIKE?

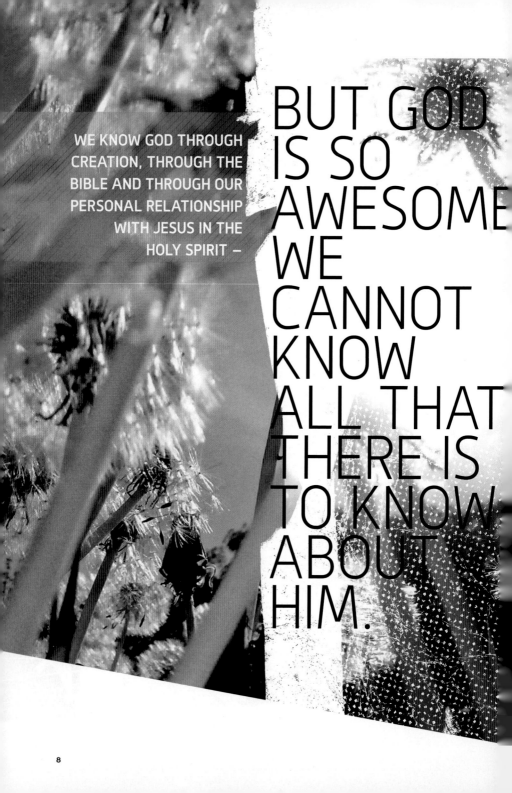

WE KNOW GOD THROUGH CREATION, THROUGH THE BIBLE AND THROUGH OUR PERSONAL RELATIONSHIP WITH JESUS IN THE HOLY SPIRIT —

BUT GOD IS SO AWESOME WE CANNOT KNOW ALL THAT THERE IS TO KNOW ABOUT HIM.

SENTENCE 01 WE KNOW GOD THROUGH CREATION, THROUGH THE BIBLE AND THROUGH OUR PERSONAL RELATIONSHIP WITH JESUS IN THE HOLY SPIRIT – BUT GOD IS SO AWESOME WE CANNOT KNOW ALL THAT THERE IS TO KNOW ABOUT HIM.

Revelations ... life is full of them. They can be good – like when your mum says to you, 'Your teacher told me how brilliant you are at maths ... that was a complete revelation to me!' Or bad – like when your friend says, 'You'll never guess who revealed his true colours last night ... I saw your so-called boyfriend playing tonsil-tennis with Danielle down at the club!'

Much of human life can be seen as a search for revelation. The famous artists and writers your teachers go on about seek to uncover (or reveal) the truth of what it is to be human in their paintings and books. The brilliant scientists we see on TV and read about in text books use reason and technology to disclose (or reveal) the true nature of the universe. And our best relationships (whether with Mum, Dad, mates, boyfriend or girlfriend) are about lifting each other's masks to unveil (or reveal) the beautiful people within. And religion is about humanity's searching and finding God ... or is it?

While many other religions do teach that humans must strive to discover God, Christianity says that God is just way too big, holy and powerful for us to ever be able to discover anything about Him by our own efforts. Now, that could be the end of this book and, much more seriously, of Christianity. If we can't know anything about God then religion, church and trying to live for God are all pretty meaningless. But fortunately our inability to discover anything about God is not the end of the story; God has freely and kindly chosen to make Himself known to us. Most importantly, He came to live in our world – Jesus Christ is God's boldest act of self-revelation. Everything we know about God, we know because He wants us to know it, not because we could ever be clever enough to work it out for ourselves.

God makes Himself known in the universe He created, in the Bible He inspired, and, most remarkable of all, in the relationship that we are promised with God through Jesus and in the Holy Spirit.

'ANYONE WHO HAS SEEN ME HAS SEEN THE FATHER.' JOHN 14:9

READ ON
PSALM
19:1–14

'TRINITY' IS THE WORD THAT CHRISTIANS USE TO DESCRIBE THE FACT THAT GOD

HAS REVEALED HIMSELF AS BOTH ONE AND THREE – IT MIGHT NOT MAKE

MATHEMATICAL SENSE BUT IT EXPLAINS A LOT ABOUT WHAT GOD IS LIKE.

a God of love and a God of relationship

SENTENCE 02

'TRINITY' IS THE WORD
THAT CHRISTIANS USE
TO DESCRIBE THE FACT
THAT GOD HAS
REVEALED HIMSELF AS
BOTH ONE AND THREE
– IT MIGHT NOT MAKE
MATHEMATICAL SENSE
BUT IT EXPLAINS A
LOT ABOUT WHAT GOD
IS LIKE.

Trinity – the point where the Christian faith and mathematics meet. They meet. They exchange a few harsh words. They challenge each other to 'step outside'. They trade a few blows. And then storm off in opposite directions. Because, if we're talking maths, nothing can be both three and one (3≠1), but if we're talking Christianity, that's precisely who God is – both Three and One! So, is there a way to keep the two from each other's throats? Actually, the

problem might not be that serious. The idea of God as Trinity doesn't really have anything to do with spiritual algebra. It's not the maths that matters; it's what 'Trinity' tells us about who God is.

A God who is both Three and One is, at the deepest possible level, a God of love and a God of relationship. A trinitarian God could never have been lonely, never have been unloved, never have been unloving. 'God is love', says the Bible, and loving is what He has always been; loving is what He has always done – Father to Son to Holy Spirit – living in perfect relationship even before humans were created. The joy of being human is that we are invited to take part in the incredible, loving relationship that started before time began.

For centuries, the wisest and most learned Christians have tried to wrap their super-sized brains around the concept of one God being Father and Son and Holy Spirit. Although the mystery remains, they have come up with some helpful illustrations. Here are two of my favourites: there's the light analogy – the Father is like the bulb, the source of the light; the Son is like the light itself, beaming out from the source; while the Holy Spirit is like the warmth generated by the light. If you don't like that one, we could think about the three different states of water. The basic substance H_2O can exist as a solid (ice), a liquid (water), and a gas (steam), so perhaps the one substance of God can exist as Father, Son and Holy Spirit?

'MAY THE GRACE OF THE LORD JESUS CHRIST, AND THE LOVE OF GOD, AND THE FELLOWSHIP OF THE HOLY SPIRIT BE WITH YOU ALL.'
2 CORINTHIANS 13:14

READ ON
MATTHEW
28:16–20

SENTENCE 03 CHRISTIANS KNOW THAT THE ALL-POWERFUL GOD, THE CREATOR AND THE RULER OF THE UNIVERSE, IS ALSO THEIR LOVING FATHER – JESUS EVEN TAUGHT US TO CALL GOD 'DADDY'.

Picture the scene. You've won an award for some act of community service (perhaps foiling a bank robbery ... or, more likely, scraping chewing gum off the high street) and it's going to be presented to you by the Queen at Buckingham Palace.

At the right moment, you rise from the antique, velvet-covered chair (with the imprint of the royal coat of arms pressed into your back). You step decorously past your proud relatives and walk slowly down the impossibly plush strip of red carpet that leads to the front of the magnificent reception room where the monarch is about to decorate you. As Her Majesty carefully lifts the ribbon over your head and lowers the medal onto your chest you say in a very loud voice:
'Ta, Lizzie! I gotta tell ya, this is one lush medal.'
It's safe to say that the Queen might swiftly be heard to utter the immortal line, 'We are not amused!' And the tears in your granny's eyes would no longer be tears of joy.

One day, Jesus' disciples asked Him to teach them how to pray. He agreed and told them they simply had to copy Him. When He began, He addressed His prayer to 'Abba'. This Aramaic word could best be translated as 'Daddy'. When Jesus addressed Yahweh – the awesome God of the Old Testament – like this, He shocked the people listening as much as your 'Ta, Lizzie' would have shocked 'the great and the good' at Buckingham Palace.

But Jesus, as God's Son, had the right to address His Father this way. The truly amazing thing is that He encouraged and taught His disciples (and that includes you and me) to talk to God in the same way and to think of Him as our 'Daddy'. And not just any old daddy, but a perfect one! Our own fathers might fail us, annoy us or even deliberately hurt us, but our heavenly Father's love is inexhaustible.

Whenever you take a moment to pray to God, to ask Him for anything or to thank Him for something, think back to that image of you and the Queen and remind yourself what an amazing privilege it is to be able to talk to the Lord of all the universe just as you could speak to a perfect and loving father.

We should thank God that He has chosen to reveal Himself to us not just as King or Lord, but as our Father.

MATTHEW 6:9
'OUR FATHER IN HEAVEN'

READ ON

EPHESIANS 3:14–21

imply had to copy Him

CHRISTIANS KNOW THAT THE ALL-POWERFUL GOD, THE CREATOR AND THE RULER OF THE UNIVERSE, IS ALSO THEIR LOVING FATHER - JESUS EVEN TAUGHT US TO CALL GOD 'DADDY'.

MAKES ME WANT TO...
WORSHIP

There's only one appropriate response to the God who has revealed Himself — it's called worship. In the Bible, when people saw God or learned something new about Him they responded in very different ways — some fell flat on their faces, some fell to their knees, some shouted 'Hallelujah!', some were struck dumb, some sang, some danced, some offered gifts, others immediately pledged the rest of their lives to God. It was all worship.

There are just as many varieties of worship and ways of responding to God today — some people like to sing choruses led by bands, some like to sing hymns accompanied by an organ, some want to jump and shout, some want to kneel in silence, some want to make up their own prayers of praise, while others want to repeat the beautiful prayers of the past recorded in Church liturgies. It doesn't matter how you do it so long as you do it, and so long as you do it with your whole heart and recognise that your entire life should be lived for God as an act of worship.

Why not find and try out a new way of worshipping God? If you normally attend a lively modern church, visit a peaceful traditional service. If you're the busy kind of person who normally just 'chats' to God while doing up your shoes or brushing your hair, then find some time to write out a prayer of praise. Or shut the door to your room and put on a worship CD. Or open your Bible and read a psalm out loud.

Just do it – worship!

You could write a prayer here beginning,

Dear Father God, I love you because . . .

WE LIVE STUCK LIKE FLIES TO A BLUE-GREEN PLANET SPINNING THROUGH THE UNIMAGINABLE VASTNESS OF SPACE.

THE QUESTION IS:

TWO : CREATION

WHERE DID IT ALL COME FROM?

God created everything c
He used His intelligence a
to create a world that is
for scientists to
understand and beautifu
enough for everyone
to enjoy.

SENTENCE 01 GOD CREATED EVERYTHING OUT OF NOTHING; HE USED HIS INTELLIGENCE AND HIS ARTISTRY TO CREATE A WORLD THAT IS ORDERLY ENOUGH FOR SCIENTISTS TO UNDERSTAND AND BEAUTIFUL ENOUGH FOR EVERYONE TO ENJOY.

# of nothing; His artistry erly enough

Imagine a world without order, a world where chaos reigns. Sounds like your bedroom, eh? But I'm not just talking about piles of stinking socks and months-old bowls of cereal crusted with more fungi than a biodiversity lab. I'm talking about a world where gravity is there one moment and gone the next (you wouldn't want to be sitting on the toilet!); a world where broccoli is good for you on Mondays but poisonous on Thursdays. And, of course, there wouldn't actually be days because the world wouldn't spin regularly on its axis. It could get stuck on a rainy Monday morning in November forever.

Or imagine a world with no beauty – no rainbows because the only 'colour' is grey; no mountains, because the only landscape is flat; no flowers, because things grow straight up and down (think flower beds full of slowly growing grey rulers); no smiles, because instead of faces we would have expressionless blobs sitting on top of our shoulders.

Thankfully, the world is not like that. We have the world we have – this beautiful, orderly world – because God created it. The laws of nature that organise the universe are reflections of the intelligence of the Creator, an intelligence that the most brilliant mathematicians and physicists, armed with the most powerful computers, are only just beginning to comprehend. The world offers just a glimpse of God's imagination and artistry – what human mind could have conceived of shimmering sunsets; countryside blanketed in pure, white snow; mountains rising above the clouds, or animals of so many sizes, shapes and colours? Nevertheless, the wonder of creation is nothing compared to the intelligence, beauty and glory that we will see when we finally gaze upon God Himself in heaven.

'IN THE BEGINNING GOD CREATED THE HEAVENS AND THE EARTH.'
GENESIS 1:1

e world offers t a glimpse

READ ON
JOB 38:4–7

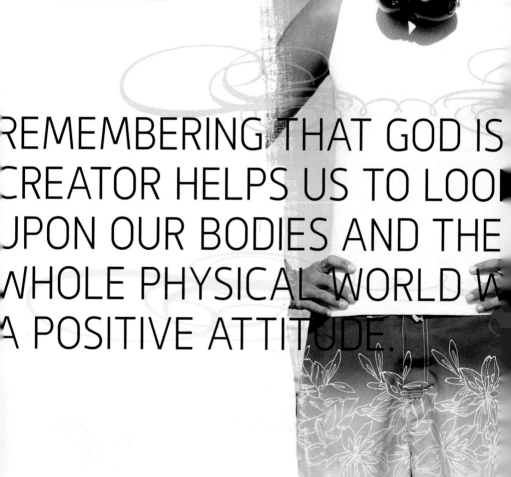

SENTENCE 02 REMEMBERING THAT GOD IS THE CREATOR HELPS US TO LOOK UPON OUR BODIES AND THE WHOLE PHYSICAL WORLD WITH A POSITIVE ATTITUDE.

REMEMBERING THAT GOD IS CREATOR HELPS US TO LOO UPON OUR BODIES AND THE WHOLE PHYSICAL WORLD W A POSITIVE ATTITUDE.

will celebrate all of life

If you were to come for a meal at my house, it's quite possible that my wife and I might split the cooking between us. Now, when my wife's contribution arrived you'd be thrilled; she'd have put together a plateful of fabulous food. With that inside you'd be full but still anticipating the dessert to come. So I'd bring in my offering, something simple like fruit crumble. Unfortunately, the crumble top would probably have set harder than concrete and once you'd chiselled through that the fruit layer would contain stones and peel you'd have to spit (sneakily) out of your mouth.

E In the past, many pagan religions imagined that the creation of the world worked something like the cooking of that meal. The top god created the really good stuff – the heavenly realms, the angels and the spiritual and intellectual bits of humans. Then he got bored and turned over the rest of the job to a lesser god whose creating was even worse than my cooking. People thought he had made a terrible mistake, placing the beautiful human spirit and intelligence in a body that was vulnerable to accident and disease, and got rid of its waste like any common animal. These religions believed that everything spiritual and intellectual was good but everything to do with our bodies was bad.

Sad to say, some of these attitudes were copied by the early Christian Church. They thought the best Christians were monks who lived alone in the desert, and believed that sex, even between husband and wife, was essentially dirty and should be avoided

where possible. More recently, some Christians have ignored the impact of our greedy lifestyles on our planet and have considered any kind of environmental concern a waste of time (their grandchildren might not thank them for this).

If, however, we remember that our Father God is the Creator of both the spiritual and the physical, of our spirits and our bodies, of the heavenly realms and our planet, we will have a very different attitude. We will celebrate all of life – the physical bits as well as the spiritual.

'FOR BY HIM ALL THINGS WERE CREATED: THINGS IN HEAVEN AND ON EARTH'
COLOSSIANS 1:16

READ ON

PSALM 139:11–16

21

The fact that God created us (as humankind and as individuals) means that He knows what is best for us and knows how we can make the most of our lives.

SENTENCE 03 THE FACT THAT GOD CREATED US (AS HUMANKIND AND AS INDIVIDUALS) MEANS THAT HE KNOWS WHAT IS BEST FOR US AND KNOWS HOW WE CAN MAKE THE MOST OF OUR LIVES.

I was a teenager in the 1980s, and one of the best teen movies of that golden era was *Back to the Future*. There is a wonderful scene where the cute (if slightly scrawny) star, Marty McFly, goes to visit his inventor friend, Doc. Doc is not at home so Marty does some snooping around, eventually finding an absolutely huge amplifier and speaker rig. Excitedly he picks up a guitar, sets all the dials to 'max' and takes up his best rock star stance facing the speaker. But he has seriously underestimated the power of this particular set-up and as soon as his fingers strike the guitar strings – 'BAM!' … he is blown back across the room by a tsunami wave of sound. As he peels himself painfully off the floor he has learned an important lesson – the more powerful something is, the more important it is to use it only under the guidance of the person who invented it.

In the film, it's obvious that the stupendously powerful amp and speaker had been built by Doc precisely for the pleasure and enjoyment of his young friend, Marty. If Marty had waited and then used the amp and the speaker as Doc guided him it could have opened up a world of fun and excitement.

Now, the last thing anyone needs to do is to tell a teenager that sex is powerful. There's no point trying to ignore sex but it's worth developing your relationship with its inventor and paying careful attention to His guidance. Sex and sexuality are not just about intercourse but about learning to live as a mature man or woman, then about learning to relate to a member of the opposite sex in a way that is emotionally and spiritually satisfying, and only finally about developing the physical relationship that can flourish in the lifelong committed relationship that we call marriage.

God invented sex and then created you and me as sexual beings. There are few better or more powerful gifts He could have given us. But, as Marty learnt in *Back to the Future*, the most powerful things require the most careful handling. If we want to avoid getting seriously hurt we would be wise to pay close attention to the Inventor's instructions.

'GOD CREATED HUMAN BEINGS; HE CREATED THEM GODLIKE, REFLECTING GOD'S NATURE. HE CREATED THEM MALE AND FEMALE.' GENESIS 1:26–27 *(THE MESSAGE)*

READ ON
GENESIS 2:20–25

MAKES ME WANT TO...

WONDER

Living in today's world, we are practically drowned in a deluge of multimedia information. From the moment we wake up in the morning and check our phones for social media updates to the moment we fall asleep with the TV still playing to itself in the background, our eyes and ears are assaulted by all manner of sounds and images. Most of what is projected at us is intended to make money for someone. But there is only so much money in the world (and for some reason most of it seems to go to footballers). So, all of the adverts, posters, billboards, brands, programmes, games, films, logos, commercials, songs, sponsors and trailers that bombard us are in competition, screaming at us to send our money their way. The result is that we soon become 'jaded' – we lose our sense of wonder. Nothing can make us go 'Wow' any more.

That's a shame. It's a shame because one of God's purposes in creating such a beautiful and interesting world was precisely to make us go 'Wow'. And having gone 'Wow', to ask, where did all this beauty come from? Who could be so intelligent as to have thought this out? And finally to realise, if God made this, then He must be incredible!

Over the next few days, try to recapture your sense of wonder. As you walk down the street, make a conscious effort to shut out the loud, lurid messages the media is pitching at you, and instead open your eyes and ears to the hidden and whispered messages that God has placed for you in His creation. Look for the tiny but beautiful flowers that spring up in pavement cracks and unswept gutters. Attune your ears to the whistling of the wind and the melodies of birdsong. Peer through the light pollution until your eyes can make out the stars in the sky beyond. And, most importantly, stare at the faces, look deep into the eyes of the people you meet – every single one is made in God's image.

What I saw today

What I heard today

MAKES ME WANT TO... 25

THREE: FALL

LET'S FACE IT, THINGS ARE IN **A MESS,**

THE QUESTION IS:

HOW DID IT COM IT T

Bad h
creation a
intende
the w

SENTENCE 01 BAD HUMAN DECISIONS LED FROM THE PERFECT CREATION AND RELATIONSHIPS THAT GOD HAD ALWAYS INTENDED AND ON TO TERRIBLE CONSEQUENCES FOR THE WHOLE OF FUTURE HISTORY – THIS IS OFTEN CALLED 'THE FALL'.

It's paradise ... you're walking along a moonlit tropical beach hand-in-hand with the gorgeous partner of your dreams. (OK, OK so it's not a moonlit tropical beach but rather the neon-lit local park, and you and your dream partner are more Homer and Marge than Brad and Angelina, but still, it's perfect ...) Then it all starts to go wrong. As time passes (and deodorant loses its potency) it dawns on you that the strange smell you thought was drifting down from the local cheese factory is, in fact, emanating from your partner's armpits. And the long silences no longer seem romantic but more like a fatal lack of anything interesting to say ... paradise one minute, just another gloomy evening in Grimethorpe the next.

Only one couple have ever enjoyed an extended stay in paradise and that was Adam and Eve in the Garden of Eden. Christian scholars debate whether the Genesis account is intended to be read as history or whether it is a special kind of myth that tells us truth about the way the world began, the way the world is, and why. In either case, the message is clear.

all starts to go wrong

28

decisions led from the perfect relationships that God had always ...d on to terrible consequences for ...f future history – this is often called 'the Fall'.

God created a perfect world and placed humans in charge of it. The perfection covered both human relationships – which were without fear, jealousy, pride, guilt or lust ... and human relationship with God – whose friendship with the man and woman was unobstructed and uncomplicated so that He could come and walk and talk with them in the garden in the cool of the evening.

But a real relationship between humans and God implied risk. If Adam and Eve were to be free to relate to God and to be truly in charge of the world, then they must also be free to choose and act badly – which the Bible calls 'sin'. And that is exactly what happened. Adam and Eve chose badly and their disobedience poisoned paradise. Their

guilt made the natural relationship with God impossible. Their partnership was damaged as they bickered and fought. And, because God had placed the humans in charge, the natural world was also affected; paradise decayed into the beautiful but also violent and unpredictable planet we know today.

'THEN THE MAN AND HIS WIFE HEARD THE SOUND OF THE LORD GOD ... AND THEY HID'
GENESIS 3:8

READ ON
GENESIS 3

I have a choice

SENTENCE 02 CHRISTIAN TEACHING SAYS THAT THE EFFECTS OF ADAM AND EVE'S SIN ARE STILL BEING FELT; WE LIVE IN A WORLD AFFECTED BY WHAT THEY DID AND WE ADD TO THE PROBLEM BY SINNING (THAT IS, DOING STUFF THAT HURTS GOD AND OTHER PEOPLE) TOO.

Before we get too down on Adam and Eve, blaming them for blowing it for us, we should spend a moment considering our own lives ...

How many of us would like to have our bad choices written down in a holy book and then read around the world for thousands of years? In the story, Eve took a bite out of a piece of fruit that God had told her not to – that's wrong. But think about it: have you never swiped a chocolate biscuit out of the cupboard when you've been told not to? Then Adam tried to put all the blame on Eve – and that's wrong too. But haven't we all let other people get told off even when we knew we were at least as guilty? Adam and Eve might have been the first but they're certainly not the only people to mess up or to sin.

The Bible appears to teach that Adam and Eve's sin is also, somehow, responsible for making us sinners. While Adam and Eve lived in paradise and had the chance never to sin, we live in a fallen world and so inevitably sin.

Sometimes people have imagined this as being a bit like genetics – 'my mum and dad have blue eyes and passed the "blue-eye gene" on to me, so I have blue eyes too' becomes, 'Adam and Eve (my spiritual parents) were sinners and they passed the "sinning gene" on to me, so I am a sinner too'. But that might make it sound as if we shouldn't be held responsible for our sin. Perhaps it's better to picture it as being out of balance. I lean towards sinning but still I have a choice every time I am tempted; that means that when I sin I am at fault and I can't shift the blame onto anyone else.

The fact is that sinning, disobeying God and acting selfishly, has been the way of the world ever since human history began. This sin – carried on generation after generation, century after century, millennia after millennia – has had terrible consequences for the world we live in.

**'FOR ALL HAVE SINNED AND FALL SHORT OF THE GLORY OF GOD'
ROMANS 3:23**

READ ON
ROMANS 5:12–14

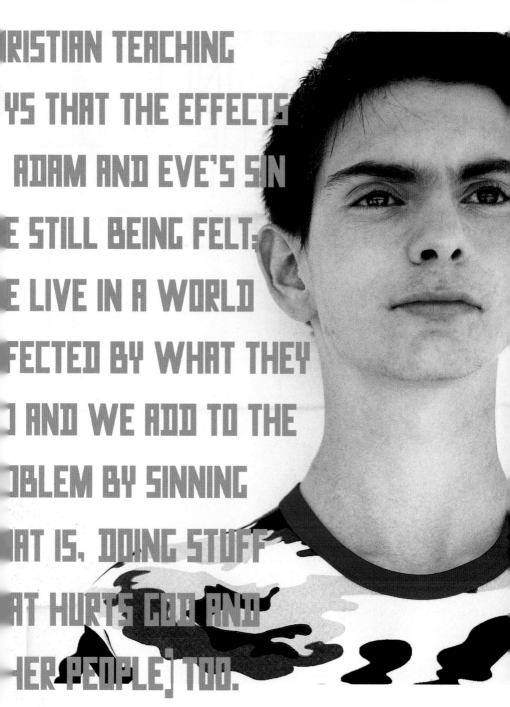

RISTIAN TEACHING
YS THAT THE EFFECTS
ADAM AND EVE'S SIN
E STILL BEING FELT;
E LIVE IN A WORLD
FECTED BY WHAT THEY
] AND WE ADD TO THE
]BLEM BY SINNING
IAT IS, DOING STUFF
IAT HURTS GOD AND
IER PEOPLE] TOO.

THE BIBLE TEACHES
THAT EVER SINCE
'THE FALL' THE WHOLE
OF CREATION HAS BEEN
VEERING OFF COURSE

SENTENCE 03 THE BIBLE TEACHES THAT EVER SINCE 'THE FALL' THE WHOLE OF CREATION HAS BEEN VEERING OFF COURSE.

destroy the power of sin

There's a fantastic relay game that involves spinning around some twenty times with your forehead pressed down on the top of a cricket bat, hockey stick or something similar. You might have played it (or if you're clever, just watched it).

Anyway, as the two teams line up to begin, it's serious stuff. On your marks, get set … go! It's like the Olympics as the two highly trained athletes sprint down the course towards the bats. Once they reach the bats they must place their foreheads on top and spin around and around and around …

By the time they come to try to sprint back to their teammates, it's gone from the Olympics to the nursery – heads loll about as if necks have turned to jelly and legs appear to have been disconnected from the rest of the nervous systems. Heads, bodies and legs all seem to set off in different directions at once and spectacular falls are the only possible outcome. What's really funny is that you can see the contestants trying to aim and launch themselves towards their teammates yet veering further and further off course as they try to run.

As we mentioned earlier, the original sin of Adam and Eve seems to have affected the whole human race so that, hard as we try, we have a tendency to veer off our chosen course and end up doing

things that we didn't really want to do, or – and perhaps this is even worse – wanting to do things that we know we shouldn't.

Some problems are caused by an individual's sin – rape and murder as well as gossiping and bullying. Other problems are caused by the sin of whole societies – starvation in Africa is partly caused by our greed for cheap food and cheap materials. Strangely, the Bible seems to teach that natural disasters like earthquakes and tsunamis are also a consequence of human sin; God placed humanity in charge and when we veered off course, so did nature.

Fortunately, God hinted to Adam and Eve that a time would come when He would find a way to destroy the power of sin and begin to restore the world to what it should be.

We will be looking at God's daring rescue of the world in the next chapter.

'FOR THE WAGES OF SIN IS DEATH, BUT THE GIFT OF GOD IS ETERNAL LIFE IN CHRIST JESUS OUR LORD.' (ROMANS 6:23)

READ ON
ROMANS 1:18–32

MAKES ME WANT TO...

LIVE WITH HUMILITY

Have you ever heard a seven-year-old telling a joke (perhaps you can remember your own comedic style when you were that age)? For your sake I hope you've been spared what's normally a rather painful experience. Seven-year-olds tend not to have grasped the important relationship between the build-up and the punch line. Either they spend an interminable amount of time on the build-up then get bored and forget the punch line – leaving you chewing your knuckles in frustration and with a head filled with elephants, bears, mice and rabbits doing ... precisely nothing! Or they skip the boring build-up and cut straight to the punch line – leaving you wondering what it is about the word 'fridge' that leaves them hysterical with laughter.

Often Christian attempts to share the good news of Jesus (evangelism) have rather too much in common with children's joke-telling. Sometimes we try telling people the punch line – Jesus loves you, Jesus died for you – without bothering to spend time on the build-up. If we are to be good witnesses it is essential we learn to face – honestly, humbly and compassionately – the pain and suffering in our own and in others' lives. We must understand and feel the force of the questions that people are asking, based on their own and others' experiences of a fallen world, recognising the part that we have played in creating such a world, before we try telling them that we have the answer.

There is a particular season in the calendar of the traditional Christian Church when people are encouraged to reflect on Jesus' suffering for their own wrongdoing, and the pain and injustice in the world. Sometimes they give up something they enjoy, like chocolate. This time is called 'Lent', the forty days preceding Easter. Over the next few days, why not have your own personal time of Lent? It doesn't necessarily mean giving up chocolate, or walking around all the time with a frown. But it does mean taking slightly more time than usual to examine your behaviour and your heart, identifying the things that are displeasing to God, and also trying to empathise with people in many different nations – you might like to think of people your own age who are suffering the painful consequences of a fallen world.

IT IS ONLY WHEN WE ARE TRULY SENSITIVE TO THE DARKNESS AND OUR RESPONSIBILITY – HOWEVER SMALL – FOR THAT DARKNESS, THAT WE ARE READY TO SEE THE TINY GLIMMER OF THE LIGHT OF HOPE THAT GOD OFFERED TO ADAM AND EVE TRANSFORMED INTO THE BLAZING LIGHT OF THE WORLD.

Think of things to examine in your life – what might displease God?

How can I help young people like myself, who may be suffering in the world?

Ideas:

THERE'S NO
DOUBT THAT WE
ARE IN NEED OF
HELP.

THE QUESTION IS:

WHAT NEEDS TO BE DONE

AND WHO IS **THE RIGHT PERSON FOR THE JOB?**

FOUR : SALVATION

Jesus is unique – both genuine and genuinely God – only He c humans from sin and ready us relationship with His Father, Go

Once you've devised your scenario, you have to come up with the best superhero or fantasy character to perform this particular rescue. Clearly Spiderman's no use in the snow – everyone knows spiders like a warm climate – but Flame from the Fantastic Four, he might be just the job. And the dessert factory one is easy – throw in a couple of sponge puddings and the Incredible Hulk could slurp his way through that lot in no time, well before the poor workers drown.

SENTENCE 01 JESUS IS UNIQUE – BOTH GENUINELY HUMAN AND GENUINELY GOD – ONLY HE COULD FREE HUMANS FROM SIN AND READY US FOR A NEW RELATIONSHIP WITH HIS FATHER, GOD.

In idle moments, when you've nothing much to do (we're talking maths exams, sermons, when you're strapped in the dentist's chair ...) there's a fun kind of mental game you can play by yourself that involves superheroes. First, you dream up some nightmare scenario. Depending on your state of mind, you might go for a cliché – the runaway train ... the lift with the damaged cable hanging by a thread ... the airliner out of fuel and about to plunge into the sea ... Or you might go for something a little more original – how about the group trapped in the Abominable Snowman's ice cave or the systems failure at the dessert factory that could lead to horrible deaths by drowning in custard?

Christians believe that only Jesus Christ was equipped to pull off the rescue that humanity was in need of. A normal human teacher or religious leader couldn't do it, no matter how great they were, because no human can avoid sinning. God couldn't do it from heaven because it was a human problem that required a human to sort it out. Jesus is exactly the 'superhero' we need because He is both God and human.

'IN THE BEGINNING WAS THE WORD, AND THE WORD WAS WITH GOD, AND THE WORD WAS GOD ... THE WORD BECAME FLESH AND MADE HIS DWELLING AMONG US.' JOHN 1:1,14

he rescue humanity was in need of

human
free
a new

READ ON
**PHILIPPIANS
2:6–11** ➡

SENTENCE02 EVERY PART OF JESUS' COMING, LIVING, DYING, RISING AND RETURNING TO HIS FATHER IS VITAL TO THE RESCUE THAT HE ACCOMPLISHED.

Imagine watching your national team playing in a World Cup Final (go on, you can do it, stranger things have happened). The star striker gathers the ball on the halfway line, sprints towards the opposition's goal, beats one defender ... another ... then another; he jinks into the box, draws the goalkeeper brilliantly, then, just at the last moment, nutmegs him to score the most fantastic goal of the competition.

The crowd at the stadium go wild. You and your dad go wild. Your sister goes wild because she hates footie and now it's all over ... Finally, the commentator's voice breaks through the uproar and you strain to hear his voice and catch the replays, but for some reason all the commentator wants to talk about – and all the replays show – is the striker beating the last defender before he broke into the box. Again and again and again, they show the same clever body swerve but the rest of the play seems to have been forgotten. Surely to appreciate the brilliance you need to see the whole thing, not just one aspect!

you need to
see the whole thing

COMING, LIVING, DYING
TO HIS FATHER IS VITAL.
HE ACCOMPLISHED.

Sometimes we, as Christians, can be guilty of a similar kind of bias. We focus on one aspect of Jesus' brilliant performance in rescuing us, to the exclusion of everything else He did. Some Christians focus on His teaching – we just need to follow His instructions. Other Christians focus on His example – He's given us a pattern to copy. Others focus just on His death on the cross – if we accept our sins are forgiven because Jesus took our punishment on the cross, all will be well. Others focus on His resurrection from the dead – He has conquered death and made a way for us to enjoy eternal life.

All of those are true, but what makes Jesus' rescue *really* exciting, *really* brilliant, is the way they all fit together. Every aspect of Jesus' coming, living, dying and returning to His Father, is part of His amazing rescue.

'SALVATION IS FOUND IN NO-ONE ELSE, FOR THERE IS NO OTHER NAME UNDER HEAVEN GIVEN TO MEN BY WHICH WE MUST BE SAVED.' ACTS 4:12

READ ON
JOHN
17:1–5

If we put together all of the different parts that make Jesus' rescue **so amazing**, we begin to see how dramatic and far reaching the consequences are — affecting not just individuals but the **whole of humanity** and the **whole** of the universe.

SENTENCE 03 IF WE PUT TOGETHER ALL OF THE DIFFERENT PARTS THAT MAKE JESUS' RESCUE SO AMAZING, WE BEGIN TO SEE HOW DRAMATIC AND FAR REACHING THE CONSEQUENCES ARE – AFFECTING NOT JUST THE INDIVIDUAL BUT THE WHOLE OF HUMANITY AND THE WHOLE OF THE UNIVERSE.

FIVE UNDERSTANDINGS:

1 Jesus sets us free from sin:

PROBLEM: We are enslaved by sin and can't stop sinning

SOLUTION: Jesus is born free of sin and resists all temptation to sin

RESULT: The sinless Son of God breaks the power of sin over us

SCRIPTURE: Romans 6:22–23

2 Jesus shows how life should be lived:

PROBLEM: Humans are a pale reflection of what God created them to be

SOLUTION: In His life and ministry, Jesus models a perfect human life

RESULT: With a new pattern to follow, we can live as God intended

SCRIPTURE: Hebrews 12:2–3

3 Jesus reconciles us with God:

PROBLEM: We are separated from God by our sins

SOLUTION: On the cross, Jesus suffers the consequences of our sins

RESULT: We can have a relationship with God

SCRIPTURE: 2 Corinthians 5:19–21

4 Jesus defeats death and evil:

PROBLEM: The universe is fallen, decaying and ruled by evil and death

SOLUTION: When Jesus is resurrected, He defeats death and evil

RESULT: Humans are offered eternal life, and the universe has a wonderful future

SCRIPTURE: Colossians 2:13–15

5 Jesus sends His Spirit and intercedes for us:

PROBLEM: We are weak and often struggle to do what is right

SOLUTION: When Jesus ascends, He sends His Spirit to His followers

RESULT: We are given power to follow Christ and to become like Him

SCRIPTURE: Acts 1:8–9

We can have a relationship with God

MAKES ME WANT TO...

THANK HIM

Sometimes, thankfulness just surges up from within and bursts out spontaneously — like when the teacher says you can have two free periods instead of double French. Other times, thankfulness is a discipline — like writing that note to Great Aunt Mavis to thank her for the spectacularly ugly jumper she sent you for Christmas.

It's just the same with our thankfulness to God. Sometimes, He gives us just what we want and our thanks are spontaneous, while at other times, He gives us what we need (discipline or difficulty) and thanking Him is an act of our will. This week, remembering all that Jesus has done to rescue you from sin and death, why not make a special effort to show your thankfulness?

Find a pen and paper and place them beside your bed (if you have a diary or journal that's even better). Then, last thing at night, just before you turn the light off to go to sleep, write a short prayer of thanks to God for sending His Son, Jesus, to rescue us. The next night you could read that prayer and add another one, and so on through the week. If you like, each night you could focus on one of the different understandings of what Jesus has done.

Thank You Jesus:

1 for setting me free from...

2 for helping me to...

3 that I can be Your friend, so...

4 for the great future You've promised me, so I can...

5 for the power You give me to help me to...

MAKES ME
WANT TO...

45

FIVE : THE CHURCH

IS IT MORE THAN JUST A SOCIAL CENTRE FOR THOSE WHO ARE TOO OLD OR TOO BORING FOR PUBBING AND CLUBBING?

THE CHURCH IS A FACT OF LIFE.

THE QUESTION IS:

SENTENCE 01 IT IS JESUS CHRIST'S WORK THAT CREATES THE CHURCH, A PLACE WHERE PEOPLE OF ALL AGES, RACES, SEXES AND SOCIAL CLASSES ARE CALLED TOGETHER IN LOVE AND THE HOLY SPIRIT.

Imagine that on the morning of your birthday you're sitting eating your cornflakes when your mum plonks a dirty little package wrapped in newspaper down in front of you. 'Wassis?' you mumble, dribbling milk down your sweatshirt. But as it's obviously for you, you guess you might as well unwrap it. Beneath the layer of dirty newspaper is an equally dirty cardboard box, so stained that it looks as if it must have been used to bail the grease out of the chip-fryers at the local café. Your heart sinks; the family budget must be in a worse state than you'd thought if this is your present.

But then, you look inside the grotty box and see a gleaming new mobile phone. The phone's so thin you have to be careful not to cut yourself on it. Retina activation means it flares into life as soon as you look at it — it's WIP, WAP and WEP equipped, it's got GMS, GPS and GAS, the processor is so fast it makes Usain Bolt look like he's running through treacle — it's state of the art!

'I will never judge a book by its cover again,' you say, 'nor a present by its box.'

The Church is often judged by its exterior – and unfortunately its exterior often includes congregations with average attendances of 7.3 and average ages of seventy-three, presided over by uninspiring ministers in strange outfits. If you add to that a reputation

IS JESUS
CHRIST'S WORK
THAT CREATES
THE CHURCH, A
PLACE WHERE
PEOPLE OF ALL
AGES, RACES,
SEXES AND SOCIAL
CLASSES ARE
CALLED TOGETHER
LIVE AND THE
HOLY SPIRIT.

for bickering over morality and generally spreading doom and gloom, it's no wonder that many young people would rather spend Sunday mornings doing almost anything other than attending church.

However, there is another side to the Church, one that you need an insider's perspective – or better yet, a God's-eye perspective – to really see. The Church truly is God's home on earth, a light in the darkness, an oasis in the desert, the people filled by God's Spirit and empowered to love one another and the whole world.

God's home on earth

'AND IN HIM YOU TOO ARE BEING BUILT TOGETHER TO BECOME A DWELLING IN WHICH GOD LIVES BY HIS SPIRIT.'
EPHESIANS 2:22

READ ON
EPHESIANS
2:19–22

THE CHURCH WA
BORN WHEN THE
SPIRIT CAME UP
THE DISCIPLES
IN JERUSALEM
DURING THE FEA
OF PENTECOST.

PENTECOST
SUNDAY IS
CELEBRATED AS
THE BIRTHDAY
OF THE CHURCH.

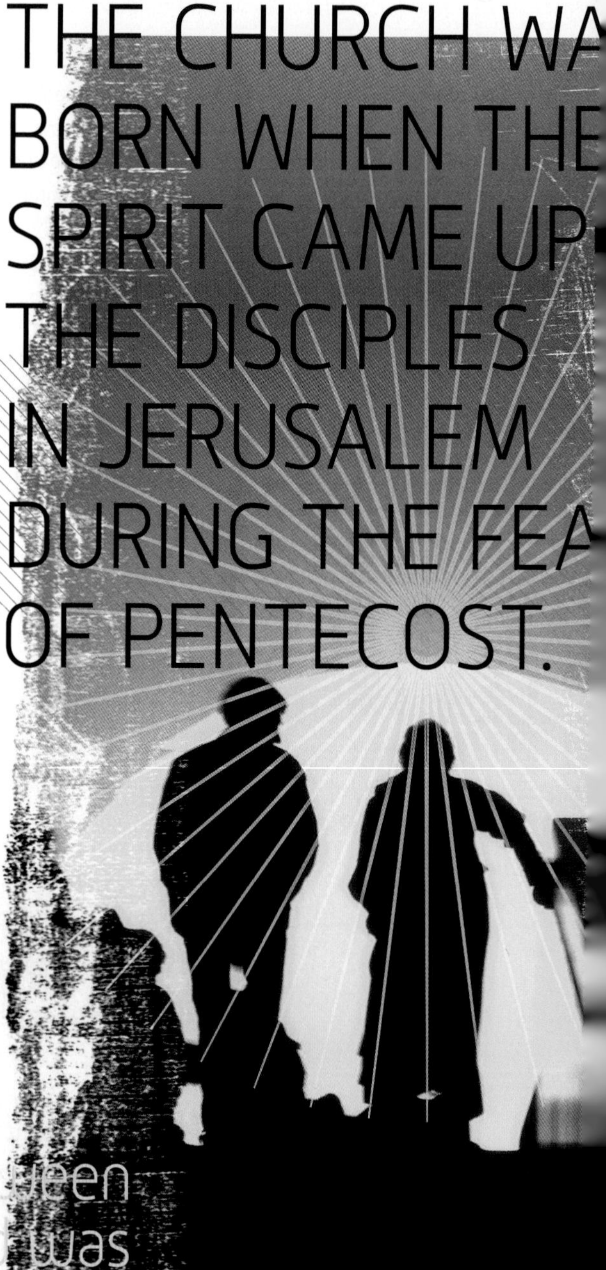

relationship between
humans and God was
restored

If it weren't for the Holy Spirit

SENTENCE02 PENTECOST SUNDAY IS CELEBRATED AS THE BIRTHDAY OF THE CHURCH. THE CHURCH WAS BORN WHEN THE SPIRIT CAME UPON THE DISCIPLES IN JERUSALEM DURING THE FEAST OF PENTECOST.

With human babies it's a relatively simple matter to decide which day they will celebrate their birthday – the word itself is a bit of a giveaway, 'birth' 'day'. So unless something complicated happens, like the head emerging into the light of day at 11.55pm and the feet at 12.05am, it's all quite straightforward – the day you were born is your birthday. But what about the Church? When would you want to celebrate the Church's birthday?

There are various possibilities. You could celebrate the day that Jesus called the first disciples – as soon as Jesus had followers there was a Church, right? Well, maybe … Or you could celebrate the day that Jesus named the twelve apostles – these were the human leaders of God's people, right? Well, perhaps … Or there was the Last Supper, the first communion, all that talk about loving one another? Or there's the day of Jesus' death, when the power of sin was broken and the possibility of relationship between humans and God was restored … Or the resurrection? Or the ascension, when Jesus returned to His Father in heaven?

But strangely, the Church doesn't traditionally celebrate its birthday on any of those days. In the Church year, the birthday is celebrated on Pentecost Sunday – the day the Holy Spirit fell upon the disciples gathered in Jerusalem after Jesus' ascension to heaven.

That decision tells us something very important about the Church. If it weren't for the Holy Spirit, the Church would be just another human organisation, albeit one founded on a very important event and with a very special message to share. But, in all other ways, it would be just like a golf club or the Mothers' Union, or a Hell's Angels gang (OK, hopefully not so much like a Hell's Angels gang).

In fact, we see that as soon as the Holy Spirit came, the kind of relationships that Jesus had talked about with His disciples began to flower and grow in the Church. The chapter in the book of Acts which talks about the coming of the Holy Spirit finishes with a beautiful description of what Church life should be like when it is lived in the power of the Spirit.

'A NEW COMMAND I GIVE YOU: LOVE ONE ANOTHER.' JOHN 13:34

READ ON

ACTS 2:1–13, 42–47

51

FROM THE MOMENT THE SPIRIT CAME UPON THE DISCIPLES AND THE CHURCH WAS BORN, IT WAS OBVIOUS THAT GOD DID NOT WANT THE CHURCH TO KEEP THE GOOD NEWS TO ITSELF.

Scientists tell us that nothing can travel faster than the speed of light and, as they're very intelligent and I don't understand what they're on about at all, I think I probably ought to believe them. But ... if there is anything that is ever going to approach the speed of light, then I think it is gossip. Cheetahs, yeah, they're quick; Ferraris, yes, they really move. But nothing seems to travel as fast as gossip.

Even in my school days, well before texting (and even the mobile phones to text on, for that matter), news of a fight still seemed to spread through the student body at a supernaturally quick speed. One minute everyone was spread out across the school enjoying their packets of Monster Munch crisps and fiddling with their Rubik's Cubes; the next all thousand or so seemed to be gathered behind the bike sheds to watch Bill and Ben knock the stuffing out of one another.

Well, the Early Church didn't have mobile phones, internet, or satellite communication either. Come to think of it, they didn't even have planes, trains or automobiles. Nonetheless, they knew that the good news they possessed – about Jesus, His message and His rescue of the human race – was not for them alone. With the help of the Holy Spirit, they managed to gossip the gospel out across the whole of the known world in record time.

As we read the book of Acts, we can trace the way the gospel message (and the changed lives and cities that it left in its wake) radiated out from Jerusalem – where the first disciples received the Spirit at Pentecost – passed through the island of Cyprus, on to Greece and eventually to Rome, the capital of the Roman Empire.

God's command to the Church: Get out there and share the good news! – is still in effect. It is what He continues to ask of us.

get out there and share

'THEN JESUS CAME TO THEM AND SAID ... "THEREFORE GO AND MAKE DISCIPLES OF ALL NATIONS"' MATTHEW 28:18–19

READ ON

ACTS
13:4–12

From the moment
the Spirit came upon the
disciples and the Church
was born, it was obvious
that God did not want
the Church to keep the good
news to itself.

MAKES ME WANT TO...

EXPRESS GOD'S LOVE

Different groups, teams and organisations have different identifying signs. You can tell a hip-hop artist by their 'bling'. Skaters wear baggy clothes and so many pads it looks like body armour. Athletes have their very own foot disease ... But what identifies the Church?

If we were to ask the average person walking along the high street, their answers might range from the weird to the wonderful. Many people would mix up the real Church with the building and say you can identify a church by its steeple, bell tower or organ. Others would think the Church was easily identified as the home of men in dog collars and black dresses, women in flowery blouses and crocheted cardigans, and schoolboys with high voices. But Jesus had a different idea of what should identify the Church.

He said that people would know we are His disciples – the Church – by the way we love one another. Unfortunately, even with the Holy Spirit to help us, we're still human, and loving as Jesus loved doesn't come naturally. So here is a chance to focus on expressing God's love to at least one person.

Ways I can help ....

Think of another Christian young person that you know who is in need of some encouragement. Perhaps they are struggling with a difficult home situation, or their self-worth is low, or schoolwork is getting on top of them. Whatever it is, nominate yourself as their very special, secret, guardian angel. (To avoid confusion, it is probably better if you limit yourself to being a guardian angel to someone of the same sex.)

You should certainly pray for them – one of the most important and most effective ways that we can show love. And you can also think of other more practical ways to cheer them up and make them feel loved – include them in what you do, ask their opinion, stuff like that. Be there for them, spend time talking with them ... just don't let them know you're their 'angel'. There are an almost endless number of ways in which you can express love for someone!

THE ONLY THING
THAT WE ALL
KNOW FOR SURE IS
THAT ONE DAY WE
WILL DIE.
THE QUESTION IS:

WHAT
HAPPENS?
NEXT

SIX THE FUTURE

SENTENCE 01 THE FUTURE DEPENDS ON JESUS – HE MADE FRIENDSHIP WITH GOD A POSSIBILITY FOR US, HE CONQUERED DEATH, AND WHEN HE RETURNS, WE WILL LIVE WITH HIM FOR EVER.

Stories, whether in books, films, comics or TV programmes, have a similar pattern, often called the 'narrative arc'. First, there's a short time of introduction where we get to meet the characters and learn something of the kind of world they inhabit. Then the 'trigger moment' sets the story in motion. The story then progresses through problems and solutions, trials and triumphs and finally reaches its conclusion and those famous last words – The End.

Let's think about 'trigger moments'. In the story of Spiderman, the trigger moment is when Peter Parker is bitten by the strange and exotic spider. But nothing happens immediately; in fact, it's a long time until he is dressed up in his Lycra costume, swinging through the city and battling bad guys. But from the moment he's bitten the potential is there for him to become the fully-fledged superhero, Spiderman. In a romantic comedy, the trigger moment needn't be dramatic, just the new girl and the school football hero locking eyes across a crowded high school cafeteria will do. Once that happens, we know that no matter how many misunderstandings or entanglements with other partners follow, those two will be locking lips at the prom before the end credits roll.

The whole of human history, especially as it is told in the Bible, can be seen as one great narrative or story with a very clear arc – from the introduction in paradise, we fall down into a corrupt and broken world before being restored through Jesus' rescue and led ever upwards towards an eternity spent in the perfect wholeness of heaven.

but the end is already guaranteed

In this story there is one vitally important 'trigger moment' – that is when Jesus rises from the dead. From that moment, we know that the powers of sin and death and decay are broken and that the future is bright. As in any other story there are still problems and solutions, trials and triumphs but the end is already guaranteed – we know where we are headed. We know who wins.

'FOR AS IN ADAM ALL DIE, SO IN CHRIST ALL WILL BE MADE ALIVE.' 1 CORINTHIANS 15:22

While Christians disagree over when the end will come, what will happen and in what order, all agree that Jesus is the centre of this future activity and that because of Jesus the future is a good place to be headed towards.

READ ON

1 CORINTHIANS 15:1–26

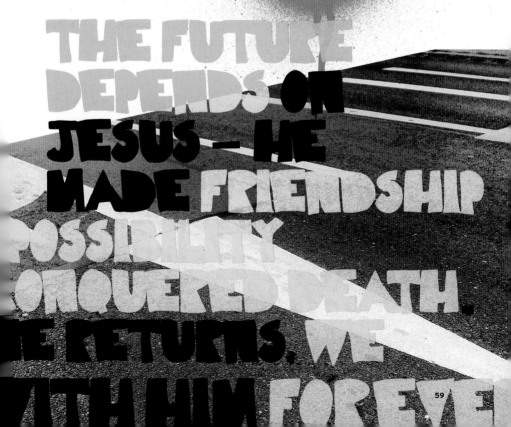

THE FUTURE DEPENDS ON JESUS – HE MADE FRIENDSHIP POSSIBILITY CONQUERED DEATH. HE RETURNS, WE WITH HIM FOREVE

59

There is something indescribably wonderful about the end of the last day of the summer term. The feeling that wells up inside you as you walk out of the school gates, accompanied by many other similarly happy friends, is a fantastic mixture of exhilaration, excitement, relief and accomplishment at making it through another year. It is a great emotional 'aaahhh' that involves looking back on all that has gone before and looking forward to weeks of warm sunshine, holidays and chilling out with friends. A great writer named C.S. Lewis used the idea of the start of the school holidays to begin to describe the feelings that await all Christians when, with their earthly life behind them, they prepare for an eternity spent with God. That future is so far beyond our experience, and so much better than anything this world has to offer, that writers are forced to use metaphors and analogies – word pictures – to hint at what it will be like.

The apostle John (who wrote the book of Revelation based on a vision he had received from God) spoke of God's eternal kingdom as a city made of precious metals and jewels. Jesus also had a favourite way of describing our future with God. He likened it to the perfect party, banquet or feast – an amazing celebration which never ends, where the food never runs out, the relationships never become strained and nobody ever throws up on your shoes or passes out in the garden.

Whichever image or word picture we like to use, the message is clear: life after death, spent with God, will be better than anything we could possibly imagine. There is nothing about it that is not to be looked forward to and from the moment we arrive, there will be no more crying or pain, no more disappointment or distress.

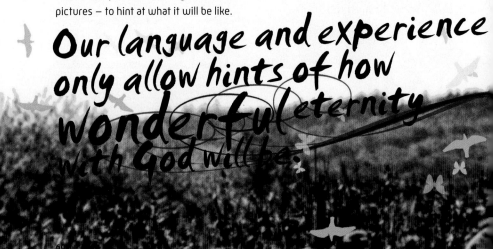

Our language and experience only allow hints of how wonderful eternity with God will be.

ter than
ything we could
ssibly imagine

'NO EYE HAS SEEN, NO EAR
HAS HEARD, NO MIND HAS
CONCEIVED WHAT GOD HAS
PREPARED FOR THOSE WHO
LOVE HIM'
1 CORINTHIANS 2:9

READ ON
REVELATION
21:1-4

JESUS HAS MADE A WAY FOR EVERYONE TO
BE FORGIVEN AND ENJOY ETERNITY WITH
GOD. SADLY, NOT EVERYONE ACCEPTS THE
FREE GIFT THAT GOD OFFERS.

SENTENCE 03 JESUS HAS MADE A WAY FOR EVERYONE TO BE FORGIVEN AND ENJOY ETERNITY WITH GOD. SADLY, NOT EVERYONE ACCEPTS THE FREE GIFT THAT GOD OFFERS.

No matter where you live, no matter how you try to protect yourself, they will track you down and find you. No, it's not the tag line from Hollywood's latest horror movie, just my personal experience of the con artists who love to jam your voicemail, fill your inbox and cover your doormat with announcements that, 'You have won! You are the lucky winner of a zillion pounds/a five-star holiday/a new Ferrari!'

The funny thing is, that human nature is such that these announcements always create a double emotion in me – a wildly optimistic, 'Perhaps this time it's true?!', and a far more realistic, 'How could anyone be so stupid as to fall for this?!' In the end cold realism always wins out – no matter how attractive the rows of noughts/pictures of tropical beaches/photos of sleek cars, the announcements always end up in my bin.

In the New Testament, a similarly spectacular announcement is made to the whole of the human race. The major difference is that this time it's true. The Bible announces the good news, the gospel, of Jesus Christ that in essence declares: all humans are guilty of sin and therefore deserve to spend eternity separated from God, but God loved humanity so much that He sent Jesus to become human, live, teach, die and rise again so that nobody should have to suffer that way; if you just trust Jesus and live your life to follow Him, your future is assured – a blissful eternity spent with God!

Yet the Bible makes it clear that there are people who determinedly refuse to accept that message. They might refuse the gospel outright, or, even if they've never heard the gospel, they choose to live selfishly. They reject every hint of the Holy Spirit and their own conscience, which prods them towards living for others, caring for others, rejoicing in the beauty of the world around them.

The future of such people is not so bright. Jesus said that such people who were determined to set themselves against Him would spend their futures separated from God and forever regretting the wrong decisions they had made. The Bible calls such a future 'hell'.

'THE LORD ... IS PATIENT ... NOT WANTING ANYONE TO PERISH'
2 PETER 3:9

READ ON

REVELATION 20:11–15

lissful eternity spent
h God!

MAKES ME WANT TO...

HOPE

The real difference between heaven and hell is God. The real joy of heaven is that there we will be *with* God – we won't be able to take our eyes off Him!

Here are some amazing Bible passages to help you think about heaven:
– Revelation 21:1–4
– Colossians 3:1–4
– Matthew 22:1–14
– Luke 15:3–31

Even though we won't experience the wonder of seeing God face to face until we're in heaven, we can still experience His presence here on earth. Many find that during worship, whether at church or on their own, they feel an undeniable sense of God being with them.

Over the next few days, why not try spending a few moments a day asking God to fill you with His presence. Here are some brilliant worship songs that you could use during these times:

THE ALBUM: *Passion Live 2013*
       – Various artists (2013)
THE SONGS: *Revelation Song* – Kari Jobe
      In Christ Alone
      – feat. Kristian Stanfill
      Whom Shall I Fear?
      – Chris Tomlin
These songs are about standing in awe of God, having faith in a faithful God, and being confident in the power of Jesus.

THE ALBUM: *Glorious Ruins* – Hillsong (2013)
THE SONGS: *Christ is Enough*
      Anchor
      Glorious Ruins
Another powerful worship album. These songs are about setting our eyes on God and placing all our hope in Him and His promises.

THE ALBUM: *Live from New York* – Jesus
      Culture with Martin Smith
      (2012)
THE SONGS: *Walk With Me*
      Waiting Here for You
      Holy Spirit
This album is all about being with God. When you feel stressed or busy with life, try listening to these songs. They'll help you focus back on Jesus. If you like to sing, these songs will have you singing at the top of your voice!

Heaven and eternity with God are what all Christians have to look forward to. It is these truths that have allowed Christians to live joyful and hopeful lives in even the most terrible of circumstances. As we face the inevitable struggles and sadness of life, we can take comfort in the fact that sorrow, pain, loneliness, crying and death are only for a time while joy, happiness, laughter and life in God's presence will be for ever.

In your times of worship, thank God for the amazing future we have to look forward to.

SEVEN : KNOWING GOD 1 – THE BIBLE

WE ALL KNOW
THE BIBLE IS
IMPORTANT.

THE QUESTION IS:

HOW CAN AN ANCIENT TEXT HAVE A POSITIVE IMPACT ON THE LIFE OF A YOUNG PERSON IN THE TWENTY-FIRST CENTURY?

GOD HAS GIVEN US THE BIBL
HAVE A STANDARD AGAINST
JUDGE THE IDEAS ABOUT GC
FROM OUR EXPERIENCES,
FROM OUR THINKING AND
FROM OUR CHURCHES

SENTENCE 01 GOD HAS GIVEN US THE BIBLE SO THAT WE HAVE A STANDARD AGAINST WHICH WE CAN JUDGE THE IDEAS ABOUT GOD THAT COME FROM OUR EXPERIENCES, FROM OUR THINKING AND FROM OUR CHURCHES.

We all have a tendency to make snap-judgments about people based on only the scantiest amount of evidence. We are quick to pigeonhole people based on the most tired clichés imaginable — footballers' wives are blonde bimbos; politicians are liars; beautiful people are the most fun to be with; rich people are the happiest. But if we actually had the opportunity and took the time to get to know some footballers' wives, politicians, beautiful people or millionaires we would find that those clichés are not necessarily true. Some footballers' wives are ordinary-looking but deeply loved by their husbands; some politicians value the truth more highly than their careers; some beautiful people are boring, and some rich people are unhappy.

Worryingly, people have always had the tendency to act the same way with God. All human cultures in all of history have built up their own ideas, their own clichés, about God — He's a cruel tyrant demanding sacrifices; He's a kind old man with a white

those clichés are not
necessarily true

68

God's own account of who He is

beard sitting on a cloud; He's a brilliant engineer who made the world and then left it alone; He's a great, fierce warrior, or He's an impersonal force for good.

Fortunately, God did not leave us alone with our confused

clichés. In His kindness, wanting to be truly known by us, He revealed Himself to certain men and women and inspired them – apostles and prophets – to tell of what He had revealed to them. Over time, the Jewish people and later, the Early Christian Church, came to recognise these writings as unique. They have been passed on to us in the form of the Bible.

The Bible is God's own account of who He is. Because we have the Bible we don't have to make do with tired clichés or vague guesses.

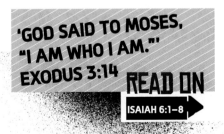

'GOD SAID TO MOSES,
"I AM WHO I AM."'
EXODUS 3:14

READ ON
ISAIAH 6:1–8 ➤

SENTENCE 02 THE BIBLE IS NOT SIMPLE. GOD GAVE US A BOOK THAT INCLUDES PROPHECY, FICTION, POETRY, SONGS, HISTORY AND RELIGION.

Real trouble can happen when you use something in a way it wasn't designed for. Some friends and I once came up with a great money-saving plan for recharging non-rechargeable batteries. We found a length of electrical flex with a plug at one end and we bared the live and neutral wires at the other end and prepared to attach those bare wires to either end of the battery. Now, I'd hate you to think we were stupid; we thought a dress rehearsal of our plan with an adult in attendance was called for. We asked one of our mums. My friend explained exactly what we planned to do and, holding the battery in one hand, he used his fingers to press the live and neutral wires to the top and bottom of the battery. Unfortunately, another member of the group had forgotten this was just a dress rehearsal and plugged the flex into the mains. The wires made contact and …

BANG!

Fortunately, my friend survived with nothing worse than blackened fingers. But it was a rather scary lesson in the importance of not misusing powerful things like electricity – or the Bible.

The Bible is not a simple book of instructions dictated by God. The Bible contains all the guidance we need but it won't be found by just reading it off the page as if God sat in heaven thousands of years ago writing answers to all our twenty-first-century questions. The Bible is far more powerful

The Bible is not simple. God gave us a book that in prophecy, fiction, poetry, songs, history and religion.

70

and far more exciting than that – because it is God's Word, it has the power to speak to us directly and to challenge us to change. There are times when the Holy Spirit causes the words of the Bible to appear to jump off the page and become immediately relevant to our lives. But to make the most of the Bible, and to hear God speak to us through it on a regular basis, we have to practise reading in a careful and sensitive way.

'FOR THE WORD OF GOD IS LIVING AND ACTIVE. SHARPER THAN ANY DOUBLE-EDGED SWORD' HEBREWS 4:12

READ ON

SONG OF SONGS 1:1–4

des

all the guidance we need

SENTENCE 03 AS WE STUDY THE BIBLE IT IS IMPORTANT TO REMEMBER THAT WE ARE NOT JUST LEARNING FACTS BUT SHOULD BE APPLYING WHAT WE LEARN TO MAKE US BETTER DISCIPLES OF JESUS (CHRISTIANS) AND TO DEEPEN OUR RELATIONSHIP WITH GOD.

If you could travel back in time to any moment in Bible history, which would it be? You could choose the epic moments – the parting of the Red Sea, the Nativity, the Sermon on the Mount or the resurrection! If you have a slightly quirkier sense of humour, you might fancy seeing plagues of frogs, talking donkeys or the insides of a great fish. And of course there are enough gruesome murders and epic battles to keep horror and fantasy fans very happy.

All these happenings took place a long, long time ago in a galaxy (actually a small Middle Eastern country) far, far away. If we are to regularly hear God speaking to us through the Bible then we have to take that distance

As we study the Bible it is important to remember that we are not just learning facts but should be applying what we learn to make us better disciples of Jesus (Christians) and to deepen our relationship with God.

know God and to hear Him

seriously. To read the Bible for all its worth requires our travelling through time in our imaginations.

When we read a passage of the Bible we can learn a lot by starting in the distant past. We can ask ourselves, what do I think the author of this passage was trying to say? What did this passage mean to the people that the author was writing for? If we can answer these questions we are ready to zoom through thousands of years of history to the present. Now we need to ask, what does this mean for me today? Is the same message applicable to me in my situation, or does God want me to learn something else from this? But the present isn't the end of the story. We must also imagine our way into the future. What must I change about my life to live true to what I have learnt from this passage?

When we read the Bible in this way it can stop being just a series of dry histories, or a list of outdated instructions or an encyclopaedia of facts about God. Instead, it becomes a way for us to know God and to hear Him speaking into our lives.

Suggested helps:

DAILY BIBLE READING NOTES:
YP's

Mettle

(for more information see pages 126–127)

USEFUL WEBSITES:
www.word-on-the-web.co.uk

www.biblegateway.com

www.soulsurvivor.com/uk

www.message.org.uk

BIBLES AND EXTRA READING:
Youth Bible: New Century Version

NIV Study Bible

The Word on the Street – Rob Lacey

The Message – Eugene H. Peterson

Good News Bible: Today's English Version

The Living Bible

The Liberator – Rob Lacey

> 'ALL SCRIPTURE IS GOD-BREATHED AND IS USEFUL FOR TEACHING, REBUKING, CORRECTING AND TRAINING IN RIGHTEOUSNESS, SO THAT THE MAN OF GOD MAY BE THOROUGHLY EQUIPPED FOR EVERY GOOD WORK.'
> 2 TIMOTHY 3:16

READ ON

1 TIMOTHY 4:11–16

hat does this mean me today?

- The kind of Bible that we have tells us a great deal about God.

- He loves creativity – the Bible uses beautiful stories, poetry, songs and history.

- He is gentle – God's inspiration didn't crush but brought out the best in the human writers.

- He respects us – God could have given us a simple rulebook; instead, He gave us a complex Bible that with the Spirit's help we must use our intelligence and our life-experience to interpret and apply.

SO NEXT TIME YOU PICK UP A BIBLE, REMEMBER WHAT AN AMAZING BOOK IT IS. PRAY AND ASK THE HOLY SPIRIT TO COME AND LIGHT UP YOUR MIND AND YOUR IMAGINATION, AND BRING GOD'S WORD ALIVE AS NEVER BEFORE.

THE BIBLE

AT MOMENTS OF
GREAT STRESS
OR GREAT
JOY ALMOST
EVERYONE
PRAYS. THE
QUESTION IS:

HOW CAN I
MAKE IT A

EIGHT : KNOWING GOD 2 — PRAYER

CENTRAL AND EXCITING PART OF MY DAY-TO-DAY LIFE?

Prayer is a gift from God, allowing us to live our lives in constant relationship with Hi

It's up to us whether we make the most of the gift.

se and intimate
ationship with God

SENTENCE 01 PRAYER IS A GIFT
FROM GOD, ALLOWING US TO
LIVE OUR LIVES IN CONSTANT
RELATIONSHIP WITH HIM. IT'S UP TO
US WHETHER WE MAKE THE MOST
OF THE GIFT.

It has been said that imitation is the
sincerest form of flattery. Which, roughly
translated, means that if your little brother
is driving you crazy — following you
around, always wanting to be doing what
you're doing, never giving you a moment's
peace — then you shouldn't lock him in the
bathroom or flush his head down the toilet.
Instead you should feel proud and flattered
that someone is so impressed by you that
they want to imitate you. As it happens,
another word for 'imitator' is 'disciple'.

The disciples followed Jesus around just
like they were His kid brothers — in awe of
His superior understanding
of the world, His power, authority,
kindness and relationship with God.

One of the key areas where we see the
disciples wanting to copy Jesus is in the
way He prayed. As Jews, the disciples
were used to the discipline of daily prayers,
probably praying many times a day, but
they had never seen anything
like the kind of praying that
Jesus did. Jesus' praying didn't look like a
religious ritual at all; it looked like the most
vital and exciting kind of relationship.

Jesus spent extended times praying
before and during all the most important
moments, decisions and crises of His
life. Many times the disciples must have
watched Him leave their camp and walk up
into the hills to pray to His Father, not just
for minutes but for hours, and then return
to them refreshed and revitalised. This was
something more potent than mere sleep.

When the disciples eventually asked Jesus
to teach them to pray, He began with the
earth-shattering word 'Abba' — my Father,
Daddy. This was totally different to the
traditional religious way of praying (Jews
didn't even dare use God's name because
it was too holy). Jesus was showing His
disciples that they too could experience
exactly the kind of close and
intimate relationship with
God through prayer that He had.

That same kind of close, intimate
relationship with God is still available to
today's disciples of Jesus — you and
me — so let's go on to think about what
that relationship means and how we can
develop it.

**'ONE DAY JESUS WAS PRAYING
... WHEN HE FINISHED, ONE OF
HIS DISCIPLES SAID TO HIM,
"LORD, TEACH US TO PRAY"'
LUKE 11:1**

READ ON
MATTHEW
6:5-15

AS WELL AS BEING ABOUT RELATIONSHIP, PRAYER IS ALSO ABOUT PARTNERSHIP. GOD INVITES US TO BECOME INVOLVED WITH HIS WORK HERE ON EARTH THROUGH PRAYER.

SENTENCE 02 AS WELL AS BEING ABOUT RELATIONSHIP, PRAYER IS ALSO ABOUT PARTNERSHIP. GOD INVITES US TO BECOME INVOLVED WITH HIS WORK HERE ON EARTH THROUGH PRAYER.

For some bizarre reason, when I was ten years old, my primary school was invited to take part in a Tudor Dance Festival put on by a local university. My suffering was terrible to behold as I pranced around in circles like Little Lord Fauntleroy, holding hands with a girl (a girl!), while an old crone of a music teacher pounded out weird melodies on a piano. To add insult to injury, practices took place during what had been my favourite lesson – PE.

I have to admit that my suffering was nothing compared to my poor partner's. Even today her toes have probably not recovered from the trampling I gave them more than twenty years ago. Things only got worse as the big day of the festival approached and we were forced to do our prancing in ghastly, garish costumes that, in my case, included short purple bloomers and white tights. Fortunately, when the week of the festival arrived I contrived to be seriously ill and had to stay at home. My partner was set free to dance with someone with a normal level of co-ordination.

our prayers really matter

Quite amazingly, prayer calls us into partnership with God. Relationship and friendship is one thing – His willingness to relate to us at all shows the grace and love of God. But more remarkable yet is the fact that prayer is not just about relationship; it is also about getting things done. It seems that our part in seeing God's kingdom come in the world is important.

The way prayer is portrayed in the Bible shows that God frequently limits Himself to working in partnership with praying humans. In some mysterious way, our prayers release our Partner to do what He wants to do in the world – saving someone, healing someone, blessing someone or protecting someone. Amazingly, our prayers really matter.

His willingness to relate to us

'THE SMOKE OF THE INCENSE, TOGETHER WITH THE PRAYERS OF THE SAINTS, WENT UP BEFORE GOD' REVELATION 8:4

READ ON

ACTS 12:1–19

It is easy to get stuck in a rut with prayer

SENTENCE 03 PRAYER DOESN'T NEED TO BE BORING. IF YOU'VE BECOME STUCK IN A RUT, IT'S TIME TO TRY SOMETHING NEW.

I once watched an interview, on television, with a man who only ate Big Macs. He was an American, naturally, and the truly remarkable thing was that although he had eaten Big Macs every day for the last ten years or so, he was as skinny as a rake. But can you imagine? Not only did he never visit another fast food chain for a Whopper or a Zinger, he never even tried another of McDonald's burgers – it was a Big Mac every time. I've only one thing to say –

how boring!

Sometimes our prayer lives can mirror that man's eating habits. It is easy to get stuck in a rut with prayer, just doing the same thing over and over until you become so bored that the very thought of prayer makes you want to yawn.

There are some vital components to a good prayer life but once we have these in place we can mix things up in lots of fresh ways. The key components are 'Thank you', 'Sorry' and 'Please'. 'Thank you' should be our constant response to all of the good things that God has given to us – also called praise and worship. 'Sorry' reminds us of the fact that we never live exactly as God would wish. No matter how hard we try, we fall into selfishness and pride. In other words, we sin and should take time to recognise our mistakes and say

sorry for them (repent). 'Please' represents the kind of praying that comes most naturally to us. It is absolutely appropriate to ask God for His help with the areas of life that we and those we love and care for are finding a struggle.

Bearing these three essential components in mind you might like to try some of these ideas in your prayer life:

1. Listening to a worship CD, singing along or just thinking about the words – **'Thank you'**
2. Writing down a list of areas where you feel you've failed and then erasing each entry as you ask for forgiveness for that failing – **'Sorry'**
3. Reading Psalm 51:1–17 and making it personal; writing it out in your words – **'Sorry'**
4. Drawing a picture to represent the way things are (eg fighting with parents) and the way things should be (eg calm discussion) – **'Please'**
5. Lighting a candle in the darkness as you ask for God's light and presence to come into a particular situation – **'Please'**
6. Choosing a country to pray for from *Open Doors** – **'Please'**
   (*You can do this online at **www.opendoorsuk.org/persecution/ country_profiles.php**)

Prayer doesn't need to be **boring.** If you've become stuck in **a rut,** it's time to try something **new.**

One of my earliest memories is from when I was about three. My father was going to repair a small wall in the garden and he asked me to help him. My three-year-old chest swelled with pride as I ran back to my bedroom to collect my high quality plastic tools. Of course, my 'help' was really nothing of the sort. I dropped bricks on my father's fingers, ruined the cement by using it for mud pies, and generally created havoc and mess wherever I went. But my father was kind and when the job was done I was thrilled, considering myself to have been a full and important partner in the building process.

WHAT AN AMAZING INSIGHT INTO GOD PRAYER GIVES US – HE NOT ONLY MAKES HIMSELF AVAILABLE FOR RELATIONSHIP WITH US BUT HE ALSO INVITES US TO WORK IN PARTNERSHIP WITH HIM! HE HAS CHOSEN US TO TAKE PART WITH HIM IN THE COSMICALLY SIGNIFICANT JOB OF REBUILDING A BROKEN WORLD.

In the next chapters, we look at some other ways that we work in partnership with God, living our lives for Him.

PRAYER

ONE THING'S
FOR SURE, WE
LIVE OUR LIVES
WITHOUT THE
BENEFIT OF
REHEARSALS.

THE QUESTION IS:

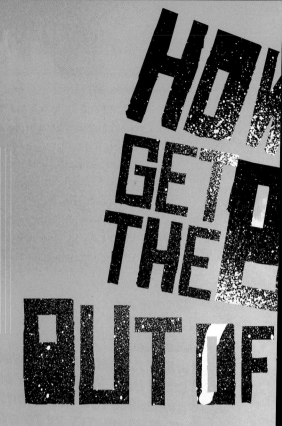

CAN I
-ST
LIFE?

NINE : LIVING FOR GOD 1 – LIFE

God is interested in ev
lives. Living as He dire
positive consequence

SENTENCE 01 GOD IS INTERESTED IN EVERY AREA OF OUR LIVES. LIVING AS HE DIRECTS WILL HAVE POSITIVE CONSEQUENCES FOR EVERY AREA.

Have you ever watched one of those old 'B' horror movies with titles like *The Ooze, The Blob* or *The Return of the Killer Slime*? They tend to build to a climactic scene where the main characters are trapped in a room trying to keep the Ooze, Blob or Slime out. Slam a door and it starts oozing underneath. Block that gap and suddenly it's coming in the windows. Barricade the windows and it starts squelching in through the light fittings … or up between the cracks in the floorboards … or … but you get the picture. Now, it might be stating the obvious, but God is not at all like the Ooze, Blob or Slime in those old movies. God wants to get in and get involved in every part of our lives but if we slam the door shut on Him, He will respect our wishes and keep out. But, let's face it, it makes sense to welcome Him in.

We have a tendency to think of God as being somehow most interested in religious things. He might be interested in our record of church attendance but not our school attendance. He might care about the way we pray but not about the way we talk to the old lady who lives down the street. He might try and call us to become a missionary or a priest but not to be a nurse, an accountant or a landscape gardener. But, if we think that, we couldn't be more wrong.

The Bible shows us a God who is interested in absolutely every area of human life. He cares about health and medicine, justice and commerce, politics and relationships, art and science, love, marriage, sex, parenthood – the lot. What is also clear from the Bible is that the way to make the most of life is to be attentive to what God says and to follow His guidance in every single area of our lives.

rea of our
ill have
every area.

READ ON

LEVITICUS 1:9

'AND WHAT DOES THE LORD REQUIRE OF YOU? TO ACT JUSTLY AND TO LOVE MERCY AND TO WALK HUMBLY WITH YOUR GOD.' MICAH 6:8

SENTENCE 02 ONLY GOD KNOWS OUR FUTURE AND HIS PLANS FOR US ARE GOOD, BUT THE DECISIONS THAT WE MAKE RIGHT NOW, HOWEVER SMALL AND SEEMINGLY INCONSEQUENTIAL, PLAY A PART IN DETERMINING OUR FUTURE.

In American high schools, there is the tradition of the yearbook – an expensive hardback book with lots of glossy pictures and journalistic articles that tells the story of the school year and especially of the graduating class, the seniors. Within the yearbook tradition there is another tradition of voting for the student who is: 'The most likely to ...' It could be 'The most likely to make a million dollars' or 'The most likely to end up in prison' or 'The most likely to become a film star'.

Now, supposing your school announced that they were going to create a yearbook and they were going to include these votes. Would you be excited to see if you would be voted 'Most likely to be a success' or 'Most likely to have a great life'? Or would you be scared, worried that you'd be considered 'Most likely to amount to nothing', or 'Most likely to end up in a dead-end job stacking shelves in a supermarket', or 'Most likely to never find anyone who wants to marry them'? Probably we would all feel a mixture of excitement and nervousness at the thought of such a vote. But the truth is that we have no cause for fear.

Our futures are not in the hands of fate

The Bible makes it clear that God is interested in our future and that He intends for us to live full and exciting – but not necessarily easy or comfortable – lives. Our futures are not in the hands of fate, our classmates or even our parents, teachers and bosses. Our futures are in our hands and God's hands. If we are willing to live for God, to hear and obey His guidance, and be sensitive to the special gifts and callings that He has given us, then we look to the future with great hope and excitement.

'"FOR I KNOW THE PLANS I HAVE FOR YOU," DECLARES THE LORD, "PLANS TO PROSPER YOU AND NOT TO HARM YOU, PLANS TO GIVE YOU HOPE AND A FUTURE."' JEREMIAH 29:11

READ ON

JOHN
16:5–16

Only God knows our
future and His plans
for us are good,
but the decisions
that we make right
now, however
small and seemingly
inconsequential, play
a part in determining
our future.

THE WAY TO LIVE A FULFILLED AND **EXCITING** LIFE WITH AND FOR **GOD** IS TO BE REALISTIC ABOUT OUR STRENGTHS AND WEAKNESSES, OUR HOPES AND DESIRES; TO THANK GOD FOR THE **STRENGTHS** AND ABILITIES HE HAS GIFTED US WITH AND TO ASK HIM TO **HELP US** WHERE WE ARE WEAK.

SENTENCE 03 THE WAY TO LIVE A FULFILLED AND EXCITING LIFE WITH AND FOR GOD IS TO BE REALISTIC ABOUT OUR STRENGTHS AND WEAKNESSES, OUR HOPES AND DESIRES; TO THANK GOD FOR THE STRENGTHS AND ABILITIES HE HAS GIFTED US WITH AND TO ASK HIM TO HELP US WHERE WE ARE WEAK.

If your story is made into a West End stage musical then you can be pretty certain you've lived an interesting life. One of the most exciting stories in the Old Testament is that of Joseph (and his Amazing Technicolor Dreamcoat) and his life has been turned into novels, cartoons, films and, of course, a musical!

In the book of Genesis, between chapters 37 and 41, we see Joseph's life laid out before us. He rises from being a spoilt young child with many jealous older brothers to being Pharaoh's second in command, ruling over Egypt, the one military and economic superpower of his day.

The story is remarkable, not only because Joseph rose to a position of immense power, but because of all the twists and turns along the way. As we seek to make the most of our lives by following God's guidance, we can learn a lot from Joseph's story. As an exercise in working towards a full, exciting and God-pleasing life, read these verses and think through these questions:

Genesis 37:5–7 Joseph wasn't perfect; he certainly wasn't subtle.
Are there areas of weakness in my life like the lack of humility and subtlety in Joseph's life?

Genesis 37:23–24 Joseph didn't have it easy; he was mistreated by his brothers.
Do I feel I've been unfairly treated or got a raw deal, and that this has stopped me from fulfilling my potential? What do I need to do, who do I need to forgive, to put this behind me, so it can't hold me back from living my life fully for God?

Genesis 39:1–6a Joseph was favoured but he also worked hard.
Do I work hard and make the most of God's favour and the abilities He has given me?

Genesis 39:6–12 Joseph had integrity and was trustworthy.
Do I show integrity and resist temptation as Joseph did?

Genesis 40:8 Joseph used the gifts God had given him.
What are the particular gifts that God has given me? (Everyone has some, so make a list of yours. Or get someone who knows you well and cares for you to help.)

Genesis 41:39–40 Joseph eventually reached the place God intended for him and was able to deliver God's people from famine.
Am I praying even now that God would lead me in the plans that He has for my life?

by following God's guidance

WHAT DO YOU THINK IT IS ABOUT YOU THAT WILL HAVE THE GREATEST EFFECT ON YOUR FUTURE LIFE? IS IT THE WAY YOU LOOK, THE TALENTS YOU HAVE, THE QUALITIES YOU EXHIBIT, THE VALUES YOU LIVE BY?

Well, here's an answer that you might not have thought of. Some great Christian scholars have argued that the most important thing about a person, the thing that will have the greatest effect on the course of their future life is ... wait for it ... the way they picture God.

So, what does that mean, and how can it affect your future? Well, imagine that your picture of God is of an angry, vengeful deity, just waiting to pounce on any mistake that you make and punish you for it. If that is your picture of God then your future life will probably be crippled by fear – you will be too scared to take any risks because of what God might do to punish you if you fail. You could end up living a life of boring mediocrity. How about if your picture of God is of a kind old grandfather in the sky, a sort of heavenly Father Christmas, who sits up there with a sack full of gifts to drop down on you? You might not be crippled by fear – what's to be afraid of? But you might find that you become self-centred and lazy, believing that life is all about being happy and waiting for God to rain good things down on you without your having to do a stroke of work. That's not the way to a full and exciting life either. What if you think of God as just being interested in the 'religious' things? You might make a big effort about church and prayer but not realise that God is just as interested in your career, your leisure time, your relationships.

As Christians, we don't just know *about* God, but we actually *know* God – we have a friendship with Him through Jesus in the power of the Spirit. But we also need to meet regularly with other Christians, learn from the teaching of our Christian leaders and study the Bible if we are to build up the picture of God that will help us towards a full and exciting life.

LIFE WITHOUT
PURPOSE IS
BORING.
WE ALL NEED A
MISSION.

THE QUESTION IS:

TEN :LIVING FOR GOD 2 – MISSION

WHAT MISSION HAS GOD GIVEN US???

SENTENCE01 AS GOD'S PEOPLE, SAVED IN CHRIST, WE HAVE A MISSION TO PUT OUR FAITH INTO ACTION AND TO SHOW OTHERS GOD'S LOVE THROUGH SIMPLE BUT PRACTICAL HELP. IT IS CLEAR THAT WE ARE FALLING SHORT OF GOD'S BEST FOR US IF WE FAIL TO DO THIS.

I don't know if you're the gym type ... but I'm not. I love sports but hate all those boring, sweaty repetitions in the gym. Perhaps it's because I never had a 'gym buddy' to work out with. The role of a 'gym buddy' is not just to offer encouragement with tough-guy dialogue but actually to help out if things go wrong. If your arms give out while you're bench-pressing huge weights and you've got a steel bar loaded with lead discs pressing down on your chest (or if you're really unlucky, your neck) you need your 'gym buddy' to actually do something. What kind of a friend would it be who stuck with the verbal encouragement while you slowly turned from pink, to red, to purple? Imagine how unimpressed you'd be as the blackness started to creep in from the edge of your field of vision, and your life started flashing before your eyes, and the white light started approaching from the end of a tunnel if, in the background, you could still hear your 'gym buddy' saying, 'Go on', 'Just do it!', 'Tough it out!'

In Matthew's Gospel, Jesus has something vital to say about the importance not just of talking the talk but walking the walk, not just saying but doing. He says that at the end of time, the righteous will be divided from the unrighteous not because of what they have thought, or believed or said, but on the basis of what they have done. In particular, what they have done for the people around them who are weakest and most vulnerable.

We are talking about living for God and have thought about how we can make the most of our own lives. Another, perhaps even more important challenge is how to live our lives to help others make the most of theirs. Jesus' words in Matthew 25 show us just how important this is, and make it clear that it is not just about saying nice things to people, or even telling them of Jesus, but it is about what we actually do to help those people – feeding them, visiting them, clothing them, generally caring for them.

'THIS IS THE KIND OF FAST DAY I'M AFTER: TO BREAK THE CHAINS OF INJUSTICE, GET RID OF EXPLOITATION IN THE WORKPLACE, FREE THE OPPRESSED, CANCEL DEBTS.' ISAIAH 58:6 (*THE MESSAGE*)

READ ON

MATTHEW 25:31–46

As God's people, saved in Christ, we have a mission to put our faith into action and to show others God's love through simple but practical help. It is clear that we are falling short of God's best for us if we fail to do this.

SENTENCE 02 OUR WORDS WILL PROBABLY NOT BE RECEIVED BY MANY PEOPLE UNLESS THEY ARE ACCOMPANIED BY ACTS THAT SHOW GOD'S LOVE, BUT OUR ACTS OF SHOWING GOD'S LOVE CANNOT BY THEMSELVES BRING PEOPLE INTO FULL RELATIONSHIP WITH GOD; WE NEED TO COMBINE ACTIONS WITH WORDS.

The last couple of pages agree with the famous adage that 'actions speak louder than words' but actions have their limitations too.

The meanings of actions are often less than completely clear. Actions can mean different things at different times and in different circumstances. For example, if a girl slaps her boyfriend on the cheek it obviously means, 'Don't you dare touch me there!' Or does it? It could also be that he had a wasp the size of a 747 on his cheek, poised to sting, and the quick-witted girlfriend was saving him from a nasty venom injection. If we start crossing cultures, things can get even more confusing. In the UK, a short flash of your headlights when you're driving means, 'Come on through, I'll give way.' But in other cultures, a short flash of your headlights means, 'Get out of my way, I'm coming through and I'm not stopping for anything!' Getting those two messages confused has led to some nasty accidents.

OUR WORDS WILL PROBABLY NOT BE RECEIVED BY MANY PEOPLE UNLESS THEY ARE ACCOMPANIED BY ACTS THAT SHOW GOD'S LOVE, BUT OUR ACTS OF SHOWING GOD'S LOVE CANNOT BY THEMSELVES BRING PEOPLE INTO FULL RELATIONSHIP WITH GOD; we need to combin

100

Similarly, important though it is to show God's love by our actions, there comes a time when we also need to talk about God's truth if we want the message of God's love to be clear. Even feeding the hungry, clothing the naked and visiting the prisoners can be misunderstood if we don't also make the most of our opportunities to say why we are doing it. Even more importantly, we should take the opportunity to explain that God's love for the people we are serving goes much, much further than just wanting to meet their basic needs. God's love has made a way for every human being to leave their failures and their mistakes behind and begin the most amazing relationship possible, the relationship that we were created for in the first place and that will continue through eternity — the relationship with our heavenly Father, God. The simple truth is that it is a matter of balance; you need both sides — neither words without actions nor actions without words can fulfil the mission that God has entrusted to us. To get the job done we need to learn to act out God's love and to speak of God's love.

God's love has made a way

actions with words.

SENTENCE 03 WE HAVE A MISSION TO SHOW AND TELL OF GOD'S LOVE. AS YOUNG PEOPLE IN THE TWENTY-FIRST CENTURY, WE HAVE MANY AMAZING OPPORTUNITIES TO DO THIS BOTH LOCALLY AND GLOBALLY – LET'S DO IT!

We live in an amazing time in history and a fortunate place in the world. There are opportunities available to us today that would be the envy of even the wealthiest kings and queens, and the boldest and bravest explorers and adventurers of the past. We have the chance to travel to many different parts of the world and to explore and experience many different cultures. As Christian young people, we can take advantage of that freedom to travel to learn more about the mission God has given us, and also to practise showing, and telling of, His love. However,

We have a **mission** to show and t of God's love. As young people in the twenty-first century, we have many **amazing** opportunities to do this both locally and globally – let's **DO IT!**

we must also remember that mission starts at home. There is no point travelling to exotic places to show and tell of God's love if we are not also fulfilling our mission right here at home. In this section we can explore exciting possibilities for mission in the here and now and in the future.

Here and now: Why not set yourself a personal mission-challenge for the week? Think of one person to whom you might be able to show God's love and one person to whom you might be able to talk of God's love (they could even be the same person). Think, pray, allow God to guide you, and use all the creativity He has given you. Is there a homeless person you walk past who you could prepare a sandwich for? Is there a lonely, elderly neighbour you could visit? Or an isolated classmate you could spend some time with? Any of these activities would be an expression of God's love.

Or, remembering that words are needed as well, ask yourself if there is a friend who knows of your faith and your involvement in church but to whom you've never bothered to explain why Christianity is so important to you or what it could mean to them?

Write their names here and maybe a short prayer:

Looking further afield: Why not check out these websites or talk to your youth leader or other church leader about possibilities for you (and perhaps your whole youth group) to get involved with some particular short-term mission projects.

MISSION IN THE UK –
Oasis: www.oasistrust.org
Soul Survivor: www.soulsurvivor.co.uk
Youth for Christ: www.yfc.co.uk
The Message Trust: www.themessage.org.uk
The Besom: www.besom.com

MISSION ABROAD –
Tear Fund: www.tearfund.org
CMS: www.cms-uk.org
YWAM: www.ywam-england.com
OM: www.uk.om.org
Latin Link: www.stepteams.org
Global Connections: www.globalconnections.co.uk

we can take advantage of that freedom

CONCLUSION

'God is love'!

That is the beginning, the middle and the end of a course on Christian basics:

- God, the Trinity, lived in love in eternity before time began

- God's love was the source of His desire to create and to relate to humanity

- God's love has proved stronger than human failure

- God so loved us that He sent His Son into the world to rescue us

- God has called the Church to model and live in His love

- God has revealed Himself in the Bible as the Father of perfect love

- God's love makes Him open to us, and open to working with us in prayer

- God's love means we have an exciting and challenging life ahead of us

- God has given us a mission to show and tell the world of His love

- And at the end of all history, we will finally love God as He loves us.

Each of these statements is MIND-BLOWING, and has a huge impact on how we live our lives. Read them, think about them and act on them!

The following pages are graphic representations of this conclusion >>>

GOD, TH

LIVED IN LOV

BEFORE T

TRINITY,

IN ETERNITY

E BEGAN

GOD'S LOVE WAS THE SOURCE
OF HIS DESIRE TO CREATE
AND TO RELATE TO HUMANITY

GOD HAS CALLED THE

CHURCH TO MODEL

AND LIVE IN HIS LOVE

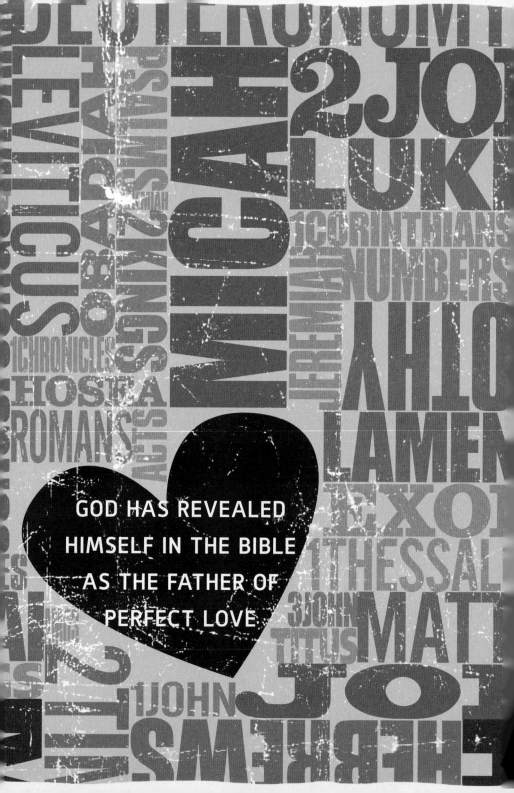

GOD HAS REVEALED HIMSELF IN THE BIBLE AS THE FATHER OF PERFECT LOVE

1SAM
ZEPHANIA
JOSHUA
COLOSSIANS
JUDGES
EPHESIANS
ATIONS2SAMUEL
PROVERBS
EZE

GOD'S LOVE MAKES
HIM OPEN TO US,
AND OPEN TO
WORKING WITH
US IN PRAYER

GOD'S LOVE MEANS
WE HAVE AN EXCITING
AND CHALLENGING
LIFE AHEAD OF US

GOD HAS GIVEN US A MISSION TO SHOW AND TELL THE WORLD OF HIS LOVE

LOVE

AND AT THE END
OF ALL HISTORY,
WE WILL FINALLY
LOVE GOD AS
HE LOVES US.

METTLE FOR 14- TO 18-YEAR-OLDS

How can the Bible be relevant to me?

Dig deep into God's Word and make it real. In each issue you get four months' worth of:
- Sections tackling Bible themes and topical issues
- Insights into the challenges you and your mates face
- Prayers, challenges and action points to help you put it all into practice.

Available as individual issues or annual subscription

Get the message and meaning of the whole Bible

Understand the who, what and why of the wilderness, cities, kings, poems, prophets and more. It makes the Bible easier to understand and brings it to life.
ISBN: 978-1-85345-512-4

For current prices and to order visit
www.cwr.org.uk/youth
Also available from Christian bookshops

YP'S FOR 11- TO 15-YEAR-OLDS

Dig deeper and grow stronger

Never did reading the Bible look so good! Get eye-opening, jaw-dropping Bible readings and notes every day, plus special features and articles in every issue (covers two months).

There's also a great *YP's* website full of loads of interesting stuff including a forum for you to chat with other readers: www.ypsonline.org.uk

Available as individual issues or annual subscription

Get to know and understand the Bible

Written to help you know and understand the Bible better, this exciting full-colour guide includes key events, maps, timelines, major characters, explanations of biblical terms and so much more!
ISBN: 978-1-85345-352-6

For current prices and to order visit
www.cwr.org.uk/youth
Also available from Christian bookshops

NATIONAL DISTRIBUTORS

UK (and countries not listed below):
CWR, Waverley Abbey House, Waverley Lane,Farnham, Surrey GU9 8EP.
Tel: (01252) 784700 Outside UK: +44 1252 784700

AUSTRALIA: KI Entertainment, Unit 21 317-321 Woodpark Road, Smithfield, New South Wales 2164.
Tel: 1 800 850 777 Fax: 02 9604 3699

CANADA: David C Cook Distribution Canada, PO Box 98, 55 Woodslee Avenue, Paris, Ontario N3L 3E5.
Tel: 1800 263 2664

GHANA: Challenge Enterprises of Ghana, PO Box 5723, Accra. Tel: (021) 222437/223249 Fax: (021) 226227

HONG KONG: Cross Communications Ltd, 11/F Ko's House, 577 Nathan Road, Kowloon.
Tel: 2780 1188 Fax: 2770 6229

INDIA: Crystal Communications, Plot No.125, Road No.7, T.M.C, Mahendra Hills, East Marredpally,
Secunderabad – 500026. Tel: 040-27737145

KENYA: Keswick Books and Gifts Ltd, PO Box 10242-00400, Nairobi. Tel: (020) 2226047/312639

MALAYSIA: Canaanland, No. 25 Jalan PJU 1A/41B, NZX Commercial Centre, Ara Jaya, 47301 Petaling Jaya,
Selangor. Tel: (03) 7885 0540/1/2 Fax: (03) 7885 0545

Salvation Publishing & Distribution Sdn Bhd, 23 Jalan SS 2/64, 47300 Petaling Jaya, Selangor.
Tel: (03) 78766411/78766797 Fax: (03) 78757066/78756360

NEW ZEALAND: KI Entertainment, Unit 21 317-321 Woodpark Road, Smithfield, New South Wales 2164, Australia.
Tel: 0 800 850 777 Fax: +612 9604 3699

NIGERIA: FBFM, Helen Baugh House, 96 St Finbarr's College Road, Akoka, Lagos.
Tel: (01) 7747429/4700218/825775/827264

PHILIPPINES: OMF Literature Inc, 776 Boni Avenue, Mandaluyong City.
Tel: (02) 531 2183 Fax: (02) 531 1960

SINGAPORE: Alby Commercial Enterprises Pte Ltd, 95 Kallang Avenue #04-00, AIS Industrial Building, 339420.
Tel: (65) 629 27238 Fax: (65) 629 27235

SOUTH AFRICA: Life Media & Distribution, Unit 20 Tungesten Industrial Park, 7 C R Swart Drive, Strydompark 2125.
Tel: (+27) 0117924277 Fax: (+27) 0117924512

SRI LANKA: Christombu Publications (Pvt) Ltd., Bartleet House, 65 Braybrooke Place, Colombo 2.
Tel: (+941) 2421073/2447665

USA: David C Cook Distribution Canada, PO Box 98, 55 Woodslee Avenue, Paris, Ontario N3L 3E5. Canada.
Tel: 1800 263 2664

For latest National Distributor information including email addresses, visit: www.cwr.org.uk/distributors